D0368851

WHAT DOES THE
NURSERY SCHOOL TEACHER TEACH?

ELIZABETH DOAK TARNAY

Revised Edition

*National Association for the Education
of Young Children*

*1834 Connecticut Ave., N.W.
Washington, D.C. 20009*

PHOTOGRAPHS
Images by Kamen, Cold Spring Harbor, New York

EIGHTH PRINTING, MAY 1975

CONTENTS

INTRODUCTION

Elizabeth Doak Tarnay has had many years of direct experience with young children, normal and disturbed, advantaged and "disadvantaged," in a wide variety of different situations.

What Does the Nursery School Teacher Teach has been one of NAEYC's "best sellers," having already been republished four times. This revision is in response to a continually increasing demand. With nursery schools moving so rapidly into the unaccustomed light of public recognition and acceptance, and with public funds being made available for the so-called "pre-school years," this pamphlet is serving an important purpose. It answers with clarity and cites specific examples of what it is the teacher of the young child teaches. It supports the idea that teaching a group of young children, whether in nursery school, kindergarten, child care center or day nursery, requires high skill, keen perceptiveness, much knowledge and true dedication. Anything less than this is unworthy of the children the teacher teaches. Mrs. Tarnay makes this irrefutably clear.

New concepts of learning—new awareness that attitudes and values are learned in the early years and undoubtedly condition all the years that follow, puts the young child in a key position in regard to his own future. And his future, it just happens, is our future too.

CORNELIA GOLDSMITH

WHAT DOES THE
NURSERY SCHOOL TEACHER TEACH?

ELIZABETH DOAK TARNAY

Here is the nursery school teacher moving quietly and happily about a room full of young children. She smiles back at the little girl rocking her "baby" in the doll corner, pauses to admire a painting and write the painter's name in the corner, opens a window a little, ties a shoelace, sees, out of the back of her head apparently, that a dispute is brewing in the far corner and moves over calmly and quickly to help settle it, chats warmly with a new arrival as she helps him off with his rubbers. She is certainly busy. And the children are busy too, with a purposeful quality to their activity. Most people would agree that this seems like a good life for the children and the teacher. But what, actually, is the teacher teaching these children? And are the children acquiring learnings that are really important for their development?

It takes continuing observation over a long period of time to see that the nursery school teacher is, in fact, teaching these young children a very great deal. Older children and adults take examinations or achievement tests in order that they may find out how much of what the teacher tried to teach them they have learned. With little children one watches their behavior when they are alone and with others, one listens to their conversation, one compares their play and all their creative activity with their previous play and activity, and in this way one gets an idea of the learnings that are taking place. For no person can be said to have learned until the new sense impression, the new muscular activity, the new idea, the new feeling he is experiencing gradually becomes a part of himself and can be expressed by him in some way.

1

*. . . they become more and more
certain of her willingness and her
ability to care for them and protect
them and be interested in the things
they are interested in.*

THE TEACHER SUPPLEMENTS THE PARENTS IN TEACHING HOW ADULTS BEHAVE

As one observes a nursery school group with its teacher one realizes that the teacher is teaching a good deal just by being the sort of adult person she is. A nursery school teacher must be a warm, outgoing person who loves, understands and accepts children.

The Children Watch Her and Like Her

The children feel drawn to her because they can depend upon her for loving, gentle care and protection. The two-year-olds and some of the threes gravitate toward her. The fours and fives look up from time to time to see where she is in the room. They all watch her or listen to her off and on as they pause in their work. They notice the expression on her face. They feel the relaxation or tension in her muscles or her voice as she takes their hand or speaks to them or to someone else. They realize what pleases and what displeases her. They sense her deeper attitudes about what is acceptable and what is unacceptable behavior. And they become more and more certain of her willingness and her ability to care for them and protect them and be interested in the things they are interested in.

We find them copying her without even knowing they are doing it. They absorb her ways of acting and her attitudes and feelings. Several three-year-olds start "helping" her wipe off the tables when she is doing it. A two-year-old fumblingly helps a friend put on his hat and sweater just as the teacher is helping others. A four-year-old is "reading" a story to a small group and tells them in the identical tones that the teacher uses, "Everybody will have a turn to see the picture." A three-year-old says to a grabbing friend, "This is mine. There's one for you", as calmly as the teacher says it and with just as effective results.

In other words the teacher is teaching how an adult behaves. Normally developing children wish to grow up and become as big and as important as adults seem to them to be. Because the teacher has the final authority in their small nursery school world, she is in a very important position with "her" children. And because she is a gentle and affectionate authority who includes all the children in her warm regard, she is an easy person for each

3

one of them to observe and copy and identify with. They feel secure to go ahead and explore the interesting materials and activities that she has provided for them, partly because they sense her approval of their doing so, and partly because the materials she has chosen are so suitable for children of this age and stage of development in this particular environment. A child would have to be very uninterested in life indeed to resist being attracted by them. And even though the teacher is not telling them what to do, nor showing them how to use the materials, they can tell from her pleasure in their constructive efforts that she approves of this kind of use.

They Act as She Acts

They observe from her care of materials, from the way she picks up a book from the floor, from the way she sews up new doll clothes for them, from the way she washes the paint brushes, that she herself finds these materials of interest and that she respects them and takes care of them. The child picks up the teacher's respect for and interest in materials. And he does this not only because he enjoys her approval, but also because he wants to be grown up and powerful himself. And here is a grown up person he likes and trusts and wants to resemble.

Of course, children are learning how adults behave to a much greater extent from their parents at home. But where fathers and mothers are away from home at work for long hours or are greatly preoccupied by stresses and strains and where there is no consistent mature parental substitute to take their place in caring for the child at home, then the nursery school teacher must to a greater extent supplement the parent's role in showing the child what adult behavior is. She teaches by all her attitudes, actions, and words in the classroom that adults are responsible and self-controlled, affectionately understanding and helpful. They like people and they find life interesting.

Different Teachers—Slightly Different Teaching

Different teachers probably teach the children in their groups slightly different things. Even though a teacher learns during her training the importance of picking up the children's own interests and developing them, each teacher is a different person with different past experiences and with some interests and abilities more developed than others. One group of children may come to realize that their teacher certainly enjoys their paintings and smiles at them a lot when they are painting and comes over frequently to hear what they have to say about their pictures. And in another room a teacher may be especially enthusiastic about all the block-building that is done and seem to enjoy joining right in with the children's pleasure in their blocks. In another group is a teacher who loves the out-of-doors and animals and insects and growing things. Her room always seems full of cocoons and sea shells and salamanders that the children have brought in.

But every good teacher keeps alert to her own responses and tries to broaden her interests so that she can be equally responsive to all the children's activities. She often gets her clue as to whether she is doing this or not from the children themselves. Such was the case with five-year-old Maggie's teacher. Maggie, a timid child who was beginning to do some wonderfully creative work and even to have a school friend, said to her adored teacher, "George is your favorite child, isn't he?" "No," said the startled teacher slowly. George was an active young fellow with many angry feelings at the moment, and of late the teacher had been finding herself continually having to rechannel his aggressive energies into more constructive activities. She continued "I like George very much, but I like you very much, too, and Anna and Sandy and Grace, and Joe and all the children. And I liked the engine George made, and you *know* I like the lovely sun picture *you* painted. It was beautiful.—Why do you think George is my favorite?" "You are always complimenting him," said Maggie. This conversation pointed out to the teacher that she must watch herself to see that she was as alert to "compliment" her quiet children as her overly attention-needing children.

Aside, then, from all else that the nursery school teacher is teaching her group, she is very certainly teaching them how an adult feels and thinks and behaves. And one can readily see that this part of her teaching is influenced not only by her courses in nursery school education and in child development and by the teachers with whom she did her practice teaching, but also very greatly by her own past experience as an adult and as a child with her own parents and teachers.

The teacher starts out the school year by making a detailed yet flexible plan for the year's work. Her first step is to find out all she can about the past and present experiences of the children who will be in her group.

What is Their Home Environment?

She finds out about the community in which she is working and how the children in that community live and are reared. Do their daddies get up at four and go to the barn to milk and care for the livestock? Do they take their lunch pails which mommy has filled and leave at six for the mill? Do they rush out at eight with a brief case full of papers that they have spent the evening poring over, to catch a commuters' train to the office? Does daddy live in another house and come to visit his child at scheduled times, or erratically,—or not at all? Or do any of the children wonder whether they had a father?

Will the child see his daddy during the day plowing in the nearby fields or coming in from his doctor's office for lunch, or will he see him for a short time in the evening and perhaps help him "fix" something around the house? And as he accompanies his mother to the store, what does the child see in the neighborhood of his house? Does he see trolleys, taxis, trucks, fire engines, push carts noisily passing on city streets? Does he see horses and cows grazing in the meadows, high voltage wires strung across the fields on giant towers, and trucks humming along the highway? Has he been warned to keep on the sidewalks, to keep out of the irrigation ditch, to keep near his trailer home? And what have these children seen their mothers do and how much have they shared in the doing?

The teacher needs to know all these things and many more about her group of children. For when the children come to school, these home experiences will be the foundation upon which the teacher will build her curriculum.

Tentative Planning for Intake Experiences

The teacher will "teach" them more about the life around them through taking them on simple excursions to see the things in which they are particularly interested, and by discussing these things with them and by telling and reading them stories and showing them pictures that will help clarify their growing knowledge of this world directly around them. She will be able to plan in general what excursions and what books and pictures may be suitable for these particular children of this age living in this environment. But she will not be able to plan definitely when to take each trip or to look at each book until she starts working with her group and watches their play and so discovers their particular interests at a given time.

Appropriate Materials for Outgo Experiences

The teacher will also be able to plan in advance the set-up of her classroom and the materials and equipment she needs in it for the children she will have. Through study and experience she is familiar with the most suitable equipment for children of this age and stage of development. But here again, after she starts working with her group, she will discover what other materials these particular children need to further their learning and she will add new materials as their lack becomes apparent.

In other words the teacher is teaching by providing for both the intake and the outgo of the learning process. Children take in impressions and ideas and feelings through their senses and muscles. They observe the teacher, the materials they are using, the other children, everything they see about them in the school and on their trips in and out of school. And the teacher teaches by giving them plenty of time and opportunity for observation of the things that they themselves pick out to be interested in, standing by to guide them as they need her help. Children absorb and digest what they observe and experience by a process of doing something active about it. Here again the teacher teaches by providing them with plenty of materials, guidance from her as they need it, and a great deal of freedom to use these materials creatively as they wish, expressing their feelings and ideas and reenacting their experiences. By this process of outgo they become more and more used to the new impressions and information they have taken in, more and more aware of possible uses to which to put materials and facts. They are really learning.

7

What Determines the Quality and Quantity of Teacher Guidance?

How does the teacher know when the children need her guidance? And how does she know what form it should take? The teacher's judgment as to when and how she should take a more active role in the teaching she is doing is influenced by her educational aims for the children and by her understanding of what teaching they have already had and how her teaching can best carry forward their previous education.

The Teacher's Educational Aims

In general, in our country both parents and teachers wish to help children year after year to take the next steps in their gradual growth toward well-adjusted adulthood. They wish them to become healthy, sound adults, who will feel comfortable with themselves, who will be satisfied in their work, who will be friendly with other people and be able to have stable and warm relationships. They wish them to be people who will be able to think intelligently and to act in accordance with their thinking, who will be constructively creative, who will be able to find contentment in life, and who will be capable of taking their share of responsibility in a democratic society and in the world as a whole.

Her Understanding of Each Child's Previous Development and Education and How to Further Them

From the time a child starts school the teacher will be having a hand in his education along with his mother, and with the other people at home who share in his care. Each child's past education will have varied somewhat, even though all the children are about the same age. Each child grows in slightly different ways from every other child and has been ready to learn in different areas than others. And each mother has different concerns and interests in her child's development and training. Some mothers and children have gotten along together very well at feeding times, during toilet training, during the period when the child was into everything, investigating the contents of drawers, scrapbaskets, sewing boxes, and so on. Other mothers and their babies have not been happy together through some of

8

these periods often because of pressures and disturbing events in the world around them. The disturbance in their relationship may have been extensive enough to have interfered with certain steps in the baby's development and education.

Developmental Status of the Three-Year-Old Who Has Received Constant Loving Care

Usually we find that by the time a child is almost three he has changed from a helpless baby who relied completely upon his mother's loving care and protection into an individual who is able to move around with a good deal of self-assurance because of his increased muscular coordination and his increasing experience with his own immediate small world. He has already been taught many things at home that the nursery school teacher will continue to build upon at school. He has been taught that he is wanted and loved through the gentle, understanding care and protection his mother has given him. He has learned to love his mother and no longer just himself. It is because he has had this close relationship with his mother that he will be able to extend warm feeling to another adult who cares for him— his teacher at school. It is because he loves his mother and wishes to please her that she has been able to teach him many things at home.

At home the child has already begun to realize that he is a separate person, that he has his own face and body, that he is the sex he is, that he has his own clothes and his own toys. He has learned not only to understand most of what his mother says to him, but also that she can understand most of what he says to her. And that she is pleased when he tries to communicate and that she tries to understand everything he says.

The child has found out that he can move things, pull things apart, investigate things. He has learned how to play with his mother and others in his family,—in some sort of a pattern, like Peek-a-Boo and Hide-and-Go-Seek,—or with some sort of an idea, such as putting the doll baby to bed "to go to sleep." He has learned to sit still for a few minutes next to his mother or father so that he can enjoy a picture book with them.

In fact, the child is learning in many ways that he must give up some immediate joys in order to have other pleasures that he wants more. He is learning that his family wishes him to control himself and to refrain from playing with or taking apart certain things in the house, but that they do allow him to manipulate and play with other things,—his own puzzles and blocks, or some of the kitchen pots and pans, or to "help" with setting the family supper table and so on. To gain the great satisfaction of his mother's approval, he has learned to use the toilet instead of soiling and wetting himself. He is learning that he cannot just dash across the street or out of his yard.

The child has also developed a growing curiosity in everything around him, especially if he has been fortunate enough to live in a home where his mother has been able to help him satisfy this curiosity and where she has approved of it. He is interested in all the things that move outside the window and on the street when he goes for walks. He is curious about what is inside of cans and boxes. He wants to touch things and to smell them and taste them as a way of finding out more about everything in this world.

Therefore, through his close, continuous, good relationship with his mother the child of three has already learned a very great deal. He comes to the nursery school ready to relate well to another understanding, warm person and to supplement in the wider environment of the nursery school the education he is receiving at home.

Developmental Status of the Three-Year-Old Who Has Lacked Constant Loving Care

Now what about the three-year-olds whose mothers, because of poverty or ill health or political calamity or family tragedy or for other reasons, have not been able to give them the constant, loving guidance they need for their all around development. For instance, the mother who must go to work soon after her baby is born to help support her family, but whose limited income prohibits her finding a really satisfactory substitute person to care for him. He may be cared for by an immature sibling who cannot be expected to be deeply interested in the baby, or by an older tired relative, or by a neighbor who is also caring for her own youngsters, or by several different people. And these surrogate parents may be preoccupied with household tasks, with financial problems, with family problems, so that they may not have on tap the physical and emotional energy to invest in the close continuous relationship with him that all babies need.

What will he have learned before he comes to nursery school? And what will he not have learned that the more fortunate three-year-old has mastered? He may have learned to be quite adept physically, since caring for himself in dressing, in the bathroom and so on may have won high approval. But he may not have learned how to direct his physical energies into constructive play nor to concentrate on any one activity, because there has been no consistent person to play with him, to look at a book with him, to allow him to "help" them, to have fun with him. And perhaps there have been few toys and no books in his home. He may not have learned to follow an adult's verbal suggestions or directions, because he has not found that these bring him as much satisfaction as his own independence. His experience has not taught him that learning with and from a loving and beloved adult is a pleasurable experience.

He may not have had anyone caring for him who enjoyed speaking and listening to him, so that his vocabulary may be limited, his syntax very undeveloped, and his ability to communicate his thoughts and feelings may be quite immature. He may have been rushed physically from one place to another, with little if any verbal preparation or explanation, so that his concepts of place, of time, of what comes next, of any sort of organization to his life, are at best very hazy. He will probably be eager for adult affection and contact, but when his interest in what that adult is doing or saying wanes (and his interests may not have been expanded beyond his immediate self) his attention wanders and he may walk off.

To build a close and sound relationship with children such as these who have had only tenuous ones up to this point is difficult. But if the nursery school teacher, and all subsequent teachers, are to teach the child anything, it would seem that she must establish with him, now, the close relationship he has missed and help him to have the learning experiences he did not have earlier in his life.

THE TEACHER TEACHES EACH CHILD THAT BESIDES BEING SECURE AT HOME WITH MOTHER HE CAN NOW ALSO FEEL SECURE IN ANOTHER PLACE— AT SCHOOL WITH HER

The first thing the teacher teaches the child when he comes into her nursery school group is that here is another place to feel comfortable and in which to have a good time besides one's own home and playspace. A teacher "teaches" that school is this comfortable place by being the same sort of warm, protective person that the mother is.

She Helps as Mother Does

When the child first comes into nursery school, the teacher uses the same ways of handling him that the mother uses, in so far as these are sound ways. She helps him dress as his mother does, do up his buttons, put on his galoshes. She uses the same words for toileting as are used at home. She sings him the same lullabies at rest time as he is used to hearing from his mother. She offers to help him eat if his mother feeds him at home. The child finds that she takes care of him almost as well as his mommy, so that he gradually feels comfortable and secure with her. He also finds that the teacher gives you plenty of time to help yourself. When you want to put on your own socks you are not rushed. You are given encouragement when you try to do more and more things for yourself. The teacher stands by the swing to watch that you don't run into it when someone is swinging. She stands by the jungle gym when you are climbing it, not worried about your climbing, but ready to smile approval at your prowess.

She Protects Body and Feelings

She protects you from being·hit or handled by the other children in ways that you don't like. She protects you from feeling anxious or guilty by calmly stopping you when you are about to wham a block at somebody with whom you are angry. She suggests, "Tell him you're angry. Tell him that was *your* block." She knows that if you had hurt the other child you would feel very worried and upset indeed, and she does not want you to feel so upset and worried. And if you have been afraid to assert yourself with other children, she helps you by standing by.

12

You are given encouragement when
you try to do more and more things
for yourself.

Maybe if you are finding it hard to talk, she helps you by saying, "You don't want Davey to take that, do you? Davey, he needs that." She tells you that you don't need to let people take your things. She even seems to think it all right when for the first time you push away an aggressor roughly. You know for sure she would not let you really hurt him nor would she let him hurt you. She helps you get what you need and do the things you want to do.

She Teaches How to Rechannel Asocial Behavior into More Socially Acceptable Activity

And when you want to do something that is not acceptable to her, she helps you find a really interesting substitute activity.

For instance, you may come to school at four years of age with angry feelings because your older brother is so big and tough, (just the way you'd like to be), and he keeps bullying you. You come to school more or less expecting all the boys who are bigger than you to hit you. You are on your guard every minute to protect yourself with your fists if they so much as look at you. You find yourself socking several people. They cry and get mad at you. Serves them right. But you feel uncomfortable. Then the teacher comes over and stops you when you are about to hit someone else. In a matter-of-fact voice she tells you that she isn't going to let you hit these people and she isn't going to let them hit you. (Well, that's good. If she won't let them hit you, you won't have to keep watching them so much, if she means what she says.) She is also saying that these people feel friendly toward you. They are not your brother. These are different people and they act differently from your brother.

She suggests maybe you'd like to work at the work bench. As you sock those nails into the wood she comes by and pauses to watch. She says with enthusiasm, "What a good hammerer you are!" And one of the boys working at the other end of the bench stops his sawing as she is speaking and looks at your work with an appraising eye. You decide to make a gun. You've never used a saw before. You try it out with a lot of jerks. The teacher puts her hands over yours and helps you push and pull it till you start to get the rhythm. Later she comes back to tell you what a good idea you had to put a nail there for the trigger. Several of the other children seem to agree with her. They like your gun. One of them reaches for it and you look at the teacher who is saying about you, "He certainly can make a good gun." Suddenly you feel a rush of friendliness to everybody in this room. You let the other boy hold your gun for a minute. You are beginning to like this place very much. You can do things here that you like to do. And other people like what you do, too. At the end of the day you march home proudly with your gun to show your mother you can do as good work as your brother (and while you're at it, you'll just shoot up that old brother to show him how big you are!)

She Builds Up Health

The nursery school teacher is also teaching that school is a safe and comfortable place by watching out for the children's health. She does not worry them about it nor does she appear to pay much attention to it. But she is alert to notice when they are not well and in such cases to separate them from the group and give them special care until their family can come for them. There is usually a daily inspection in nursery schools which is carried out casually and without any feeling of concern on the part of the adults doing it, so that the child has no feeling that he is not a perfectly all right person. Many schools provide vitamins for the children, to fill out the home diet. They require information on the doctor's periodic check-up of each child and the teacher reads these reports to be alert to the special health needs of each child,—for instance, which ones may have allergies that require special foods. They provide nourishing well-balanced meals and snacks.

He Feels Worthwhile to the Teacher

Not only is this helping the child build up a good sturdy body, it is also teaching him that adults are people who care about him. If the child learns that the world is filled with people who care about him, this is a pattern of adult behavior that becomes part of him and is the first step toward his eventually becoming an adult who cares about other people.

As the teacher broadens the child's social awareness by teaching him that there is another person who cares for him and is interested in him besides those in his family, and that there is another place where he can be secure and happily active besides home, she is also teaching him that he is a worthwhile individual.

THE TEACHER SUPPLEMENTS THE PARENTS IN TEACHING EACH CHILD WHAT TO THINK OF HIMSELF— THAT HE IS A WORTHWHILE PERSON

It takes a young child quite a few years of growing to begin to picture himself as a separate person able to do and to think for himself. And all the time he is building up this picture of himself, the adults and other children in his life are influencing the sort of picture he is getting by the way they talk about him and the way they treat him. They are teaching him what to think of himself. We have already said that his teachers and parents wish him to become a well-adjusted adult who is comfortable with himself. They do not wish him to be a person who is dissatisfied with himself or who is always struggling to be like somebody else. They do not wish him to be constantly anxious as to whether or not he is being grown-up enough. They do not wish him to be always fearful of displeasing someone with his behavior, even though they realize that he is in general doing what will win their approval. Nor do they wish him to be constantly bucking adults in an immature way, trying to do just what *he* wants to do that minute. If they are consistent with him, so that he is sure what they approve of and what they disapprove of, if they give their approval generously and honestly, then he will not need to worry continually about whether he will be praised or disapproved of. He can put his energies to better use.

They know that, if he is to become a self-assured person who can become more and more independent of them as he matures, he must have a feeling of his own power and worth built up by them steadily from the very beginning of his life. Therefore, the nursery school teacher shows each child that she considers him to be a fine person and a capable person. And she stands ready to help him expand his powers whenever he needs her help. She does not make remarks about his being too fat or too thin or too rough or too shy. She does not even make these remarks to other people where the child might hear her.

When she needs to forbid his doing something that will hurt himself or others, or that interferes too greatly with the group

living, she still accepts and understands his reasons for behaving thus. She helps him to find a more socially acceptable way
of acting that will still fit in with his desires and reasons as much
as possible. For instance, three-year-old Joan threw a shovelful
of sand into little Ruthie's face. As Ruth bursts into loud and
angry wails, Joan looks at her with scientific coldness and gets
another shovelful ready to hurl. The teacher has arrived at the
scene and is apparently aware of what has gone on. She gently
and firmly restrains the shovel. As she holds Ruth on her lap
and wipes her off, she helps her with her anger and hurt feelings by saying, "You didn't like that did you? Ruthie didn't like·
that, Joan." Ruthie is able to stop crying and say vehemently,
"Ruthie not like that." Did Ruthie take some of your dishes?" the
teacher continues. Joan nods her head, "Yes." "Well, I don't
think Ruthie knew you were still using those dishes." Ruthie
nods "No." "Ruthie, you ask Joan when you need some of her
dishes. Can she use these, Joan?" Joan grabs them and then
hands one back to Ruthie. "Joan doesn't like people to take her
dishes." Ruthie is sitting back in the sandbox, her equanimity
restored. The teacher puts her arm around Joan for a minute,
too. She knows that Joan has a little sister at home who takes a
lot of her mother's time and who is just beginning to walk
about and take Joan's toys and possessions. Joan's cold face re-
laxes a little as she leans against the teacher. The teacher does
not tell her she should be a big girl or that she should say
she's sorry; (she isn't sorry). She just accepts Joan the way she is
and offers her a more socially acceptable way to act. Joan can
still feel like a worthwhile person. And she is learning that the
teacher talks about angry feelings. Maybe the next time Joan is
angry at Ruthie, she will tell her so the way the teacher does,
instead of throwing sand at her. And as the teacher builds up a
closer friendship with Joan, she will become more definite with
her and say in a kindly way, "Don't throw sand at her. You
can *tell* her you don't like her to take your things."

Teaching the Group While Working with Individuals

The teacher has been teaching some of the other children in
the group, too, through this incident. Because when Ruthie
started crying, many children looked up from their work to see
what was going to happen. Some wandered over to watch in-

tently. Nearly all of them at one time or another had been physically assaulted like Ruthie. And nearly all had hurt others or wanted to like Joan. So, through the teacher's actions and tone of voice and words, they were all learning what she felt about their kind of behavior.

For one thing the teacher showed them that she felt individuals are worthwhile enough to protect and care for. And for another, that she felt individuals are worthy of affection and respect even if they have not as yet learned to talk about their angry feelings rather than letting them burst out. Because every one has angry feelings. Education should show you ways of expressing them that won't hurt others or yourself.

The teacher may feel that Johnny needs to be healthier, that Alec would be happier if he could fit into the group play without so many quarrels, that Cora would be more satisfied with her work if she would put just a little more effort into it, that Sam would enjoy the world a little bit more if he could be more observant or more openly curious. She will keep these areas for growth in her mind as she thinks of each child during the year. But she does not let them keep her from accepting each one wholeheartedly the way he is now. She knows that growth is very gradual. And she knows that if a child can feel accepted and worthwhile at each stage of his growth, he can enter wholeheartedly into using his senses and his muscles and his brain to their fullest capabilities at that stage. And this will be the best foundation he can lay for going on to more mature behavior.

Some Parents May Pick Up from the Teacher a Greater Respect for Their Child

Every teacher has many children in her group who are already learning from their families that they are fine worthwhile children. All she needs to do with these youngsters is to continue building up their feeling of worthwhileness. But with others, the teacher will find that she cannot get very far in teaching them that they are important, worthwhile individuals until she has helped their parents. The parents may not have shown the child how much they appreciate his individual worth. They may be openly dissatisfied with him in some respects. Maybe they do not understand the various stages a child goes through as he is growing up. Through talks with the teacher and discussions at parent meetings they come to understand better the behavior of children at different ages.

As a parent gets to know her child's teacher, in chats with her when she is bringing or calling for her child at school, or in the longer scheduled conferences that parents and teachers have at stated intervals throughout the year, she finds that this is a friendly, understanding person who really likes her child. The teacher tells her about specific good work the child has done, praises a block building he has left up to show her and points out its symmetrical balance, remarks on how well he handled the cooking utensils when they were making apple sauce today. And the teacher shows each mother her appreciation of the good ways in which she is handling her child. "Tommy knows how to manage himself so well in cooking. He can even break eggs with poise. And he has such a feeling of grown-upness when he does it. You must give him a lot of opportunity to help you in the kitchen." And the mother explains how she manages to allow time for Tommy's help with her cooking, which is information

. . . the teacher is teaching by providing the right materials and long
spaces of unhurried time in which
her children can learn how to use
their bodies.

the teacher is glad to have. It may be of use to other mothers. To another mother the teacher may say, "You certainly seem to have handled Judy's eating well. She has such a pleasant, social time at lunch and seems to enjoy her food." A mother who may have felt a good many dissatisfactions with her child often begins to see good points in him that she never recognized before. She may find that some of the teacher's suggestions as to toys and books and ways of handling him are of really practical help to her. In such instances the teacher is teaching the parent. But by helping her even in slight instances to have a better relationship with her child, she is indirectly teaching the child also, and helping him to build up a more wholesome picture of himself and of the adults in his life.

THE TEACHER TEACHES GOOD WORK HABITS— COMPETENCE AND SATISFACTION IN WORK

Part of the child's feeling of worthwhileness comes about through his growing awareness of himself as a person who can do things successfully.

Through Providing Materials and Activities with Which a Child Can Be Successful

The teacher sets the stage for this by equipping the nursery school classroom with the furniture and materials that the child can manage himself. For instance, the hooks on his coat cubby are at a height that he can easily reach when he hangs up his clothes. The saws at the work bench are kept sharpened, and the lumber on hand is soft wood, white pine probably. The work bench is the right height for him, around 24″ or less, so that when he works there, he will really be able to saw through a piece of wood by himself. The doll clothes have large arm holes that he can slip over a doll's arms and large buttons and button holes and zippers that even his immature coordination can manage.

There are many large pieces of equipment such as the large hollow blocks, 4′ × 6″ boards, baby carriages, wagons, swings, climbing equipment, that give him a chance to use his whole body in a way that is fun and is helping him to develop the strength and coordination of his large muscles. There is also plenty of equipment that makes use of his smaller muscles—unit blocks, doll corner equipment, art materials and so on.

Here the teacher is teaching by providing the right materials and long spaces of unhurried time in which her children can learn how to use their bodies. They are continuing to learn about themselves and what they can do. Through repeated use of their bodies with this material they are learning how to control their muscles and make them do more and more what they want them to do. Some will be able to get sand into a pail and food into their mouths without a spill when they are two. Some will be able to jump alone on the teeter board at three. Some will be able to skip at five, and some even at three. But they will all be gaining power and control over their own bodies. And accompanying this will be a feeling of competence and satisfaction in the mastery of new skills. We wish this feeling to become a part of them, so they will approach all new work with the eager interest that will lead to developing skill in that work. They will also be learning how to control the materials they are using. The teacher, by her smiling attention to the child's work, shows him that she is enjoying with him his increasing skill and creativeness. She is giving educational guidance in this way, even though she may be saying hardly a word.

Many children watch others for quite a while before tackling new activities themselves. Often when they start, it is by copying another child or the teacher. This is a way of learning and is not discouraged by the teacher. Rather it is approved of, for as the child uses and feels at home with the medium, his own feelings and ideas take over. And if he feels competent and worthwhile, he will become absorbed and concentrated in his own work and pleased with what he accomplishes. He will be developing good work habits.

Through Really Interested Approval of Child's Work

Some children may avoid settling down to work. Often these are children who do not have a feeling of worthwhileness, or who, for some reason or other, feel that their mother finds them or the work they do unsatisfactory. The teacher tries to fill in this educational lack for the child at the same time that she is trying

to help the mother, if possible, to become more aware of children's feelings and needs. She must try to teach such children that they are worthwhile to her, that she is very happy to have them in her group, that she finds the work they do highly satisfactory, and that she is pleased when they branch out into freer effort, using more of their abilities. She makes them feel at ease in the many ways we have already mentioned. She starts praising their work that they really do well. A teacher's praise is always honest and, therefore, meaningful to the children.

Jackie Who Didn't Paint

For instance, Miss Brown paid a good deal of attention to four-year-old Jackie's slow and cautious block-building. "How nicely you've fixed that!" "I certainly like the way you've put those curvy blocks across for the roof." "Isn't this a good store Jackie has built", with a tone of discovery, "Why Ellen, I bet he would have the milk you need for that big family in your house" —as a means of helping him into contact with another child. Block-building was the only activity Jackie would at first undertake in school, and he did a very unenthusiastic job of even that.

Jackie's mother was an artist, who was unusual in that she considered children's paintings to be rather poor stuff. She made no effort to hide these feelings from her children. Besides this, Jackie was, or had become, a rather thin, sickly-looking little boy. He did not seem to satisfy his mother in any way—not nearly so much as his older brothers did. He was very passive in school. Miss Brown gave him a chance to help her with serving lunch, with getting out the cots and the covers, with feeding the rabbits, and with many other room activities so that she could build up a warm friendship with him.

He gradually branched out from block-building into other activities, but he would never attempt painting. Occasionally the teacher would suggest there was a place at the easel he might have, but he shied away from it. So one day she casually and energetically approached the easel with Jackie and cheerfully said, "Now, today, let's make a picture and I'll help you." Without waiting for him to say no, she dipped his brush in one of the colors and gently handed it to him. He drew back. She asked if she should start the picture, to which he acquiesced. So she painted a line and then handed him the brush, asking, "Do you want to use this color or another one?" He used the same color for a line and showed a glimmer of interest as he did so. "Gee, that's nice isn't it?" said the teacher. And as he paused, "Where will you make the next one?" Jackie went on with his painting. He handed the brush back to the teacher for a time or two, but she was able to have him do the greater part of the work. He was even interested in doing another picture that day, and during the process of his making this, Miss Brown was able to attend to some other children and then come back. Jackie painted quite a bit after this. Very few children need quite so much encouragement as this.

And why was Miss Brown so anxious to introduce Jackie to new materials? Not because she wanted to prepare him to be an artist. But because she wanted him to learn that it is safe to try new activities, and when you do try them, you have opened up a whole new field of very satisfying work for yourself.

Other People Do Good Work Too

A teacher does not set models of creative work for children to copy. What they will copy are her enthusiasm and her interest in the materials. Gradually they will copy her in noticing and being enthusiastic about the work of other children in the class. Here we see that the teacher is also teaching the child to become less egocentric and more aware of other people indirectly through her own attitude about everybody's work.

At some moments the teacher is quite direct in helping children to become aware of other people's work, as for instance at the lunch table when they look around the room and talk about the fine pictures on the wall. Or when she might suggest that Alice help Kathy at the workbench "because she is such a good hammerer."

Through Accepting Child's Own Creative, Constructive Efforts

The teacher, of course, accepts what the children produce. She does not have any idea that their work bench products or paintings or clay objects have to "look like something" to be good work. She knows that as children gain experience and as their muscles develop, their art work will probably tend to become more realistic at about five or six years of age. She knows that when a three-year-old is at the work bench he will mostly be interested in hammering nails into wood or nailing pieces of wood together or just sawing wood in pieces without making anything.

For young children usually approach new materials by manipulating them freely without any efforts at first to do anything special with the medium. Very often after they have done a good deal of experimenting with and finding out about the material and their muscles in connection with it, they may one day recognize that what they have in front of them looks like something they have seen elsewhere, and they are ecstatic to find that they have "made something."

A few three-year-olds are sitting around a table pounding,

patting, rolling, and punching clay. Cathy picks up a piece she has rolled out. "A wild worm!" she announces with pleasure to the children and teacher sitting with her. Bobby pounds his round flat piece, saying, "A birthday cake!" He then pries it up from the clay board with a tongue depressor and holds it on the flat of his palm. It droops on either side. Susan looks at it and a great light comes into her face, "A saddle!" she says.

Through Involving Children in the Care of Materials

What teaching is the teacher doing here? First she has provided the clay—just damp enough to be nicely pliable. She keeps it in a special jar on a special shelf that the children can reach. The clay boards are beside it. The children help her get out the amount they will use and they help her put it away. By the time they are four many of them will do this by themselves. Then while they are using it, she tries to spend a good deal of time really observing the work of each child and making comments of pleasure and approval. If necessary, she sets limits, as when a child who makes a ball of clay starts throwing it around the room. The teacher shows him that clay cannot be used for this purpose, but that he can either use the clay at the table, or if he wishes to throw something, use a bean bag or ball.

Children bring their own past experiences into being again with the materials they are using. None of the three-year-olds at the clay table recognized a saddle, except the little girl whose father was a riding instructor.

Through Encouraging Each Child to Represent His Own Ideas in His Own Way

As their experiences increase and their power over the classroom materials becomes better coordinated, they will start planning the work they do. The teacher is interested to see what the product shows of the child's interests, his perceptiveness, and of his own individual thought about his experiences (imagination, we call this). Even when a product has been planned, its meaning to the child who made it is not always evident to the teacher or the other children. The curious teacher may gain some insight by asking the child casually, "Do you have something to tell me about it?" after remarking on, "How nice that dark blue and light green are together" or "What interesting dots and lines you have there." Children realize that the teacher is interested in this work. They also pick up her interest in each other's work. One group of "old fours" while eating lunch were admiring their paintings hung around the room. (For the teacher teaches respect for their own and each other's good efforts by hanging up the children's paintings and crayon drawings, and changing them frequently, so that each child's work is seen often.) The teacher had admired aloud the gay colors in Linda's picture. (It looked to her like a sort of ladder.) Tommy turned to Linda and said, "That's good Linda. I didn't know you could paint so good! What is it?" "It's a ferry boat", said Linda, very pleased with Tommy's praise. Tommy looked at it hard and said, "Oh." Children are well able to accept each other's explanations unless the adults and other children about them have pressured them into thinking that their products must represent something specific that others can always understand. Actually Linda's picture did represent the ferry as the teacher knew from having watched Linda on the ferry boat trip the group had taken the week before. On this trip Linda was very interested in the Captain. She looked up at him standing by the wheel in the pilot house. When the ferry stopped, he came down the steps from the pilot house and she followed him to the other end of the ferry and watched him go up the steps to the pilot house at that end. She had wanted to follow him up, but he had told her it was such a busy day that no visitors were allowed up into the pilot house. Since Tommy was still looking at the picture the teacher asked, "Is that the part where the steps went up to the pilot house Linda?" and Linda said "Yes." Tommy said "oh" again.

As we have already said, children learn about the world around them by observing the parts of it that are of significance to them and then by doing something active about their observation. Their impressions have often been accompanied by strong emotions. Sometimes the child has been confused by too many impressions pounding in on him all at once. Sometimes these confusions and emotions distort the experience greatly as he thinks it over. Vivid fantasy goes on in his mind and comes out in his play, his stories, his paintings, all he does.

Watching and Listening to Know Her Children Better

The teacher allows the child to express his fantasy freely. It is thus that she begins to understand the problems he is trying to solve, his confusions, his anxieties. Then she can gradually reassure him and straighten out his confusions.

Were she to make him feel guilty about his fantasies, or to ridicule or disparage them, she might stifle his thinking and his intellectual development. She would definitely be limiting her own means of finding out more about him. And it is only by knowing him well and the kind of thinking he is doing that she can be of most educational use to him.

For the teacher is introducing the child to the realities of the culture into which he was born. Because a young child's experiences are so limited, he is not at all sure where reality starts and the make-believe stops (even though he may appear to do so at first glance). This was vividly pointed out to one teacher by Alice, a four-year-old girl in her group. Alice had unfortunately been taken by some friends to see the movie "Snow-White", which like most movies is much too confusing for a young child to learn from or even to enjoy. Alice really scared her classmates, some of whom were almost six years old, by cutting a round "apple" out of paper, coloring it, and thrusting it at them saying, "Here's a poison apple. Take a bite." The others drew back and looked to the teacher in a questioning way for her reassurance, which she gave over and over, that this was not real and not something to be afraid of. Alice had been scared and threatened by the movie. By taking the threatening role herself in her play, she was probably trying to feel more powerful and less scared. But Alice had plenty of her own problems to work on already,— a rushed mother, no father, no real friends in school,—without having this fantastic story mixed in with the anxieties she already had. It is not helpful to little children to be subjected to confusing or scary stories or situations. The teacher does not wish to be the aggressive person who knowingly exposes children to such an experience when it can be avoided.

Through Building up the Child's Interest in His Work

Sometimes the teacher tries to help certain children put more thought and effort into their work. She may have in her group a child who has been in nursery school a year before, who is alert and intelligent, whose muscular coordination is good, but who is still doing very immature work for his age and stage of development. It often happens that this is a child who is anxious about something that is happening at home, so that he cannot really put his mind on his work at school. Or he may be upset by something in the school situation.

The teacher may enlist the help of the school social worker or parent consultant to help the child's mother and herself to understand him better and know better how to relieve his anxiety. She also makes every effort to strengthen her friendship with him. And when she feels that he is friendly and trusting with her she may suggest he work a little longer on this picture or at that block building.

Robbie was like this. He had just turned five. One day he knocked together a hasty truck at the work bench, a piece of wood with four wheels. He was about to wander off aimlessly, leaving the tools in disarray and his truck unattended. Two skills a teacher develops are the intuition as to what is going to happen next and the technique for preventing mishaps before they occur. It would have been a mishap in this instance for Robbie to have left his work so soon. He didn't seem satisfied or pleased with it, he was not going to do anything with what he had made, and knowing Robbie, he would be getting into a quarrel with somebody else if allowed to wander unhappily and at loose ends. So just as he took his first step from the bench, the teacher reached him and quietly and with great enthusiasm in her voice remarked on the fine truck he was making "What sort of truck is this?" Robbie was only slightly interested but he turned back, paused and then said, "It's a diesel." "Let's see", said the teacher reflectively as she held it and turned it about. "Which end is the engine? And what could you use for the engine?" She started rummaging in the box of scrap wood standing beside the bench as Robbie pointed out the engine and leaned over the box with her. He found an oblong piece suitable for the engine. "And do you know, I believe I've got something good for the exhaust pipe for that engine. You be attaching the engine while I look." Robbie really looked interested by this time. He nailed on the engine with great skill while the teacher got out a box of odds and ends that she could not live without. She found an old tin pea shooter left in the nursery school by somebody's older brother one time. Robbie was delighted. He cut it down to the right length with a screw driver and hammer. Then it became evident that his truck must have sides to which to attach the exhaust pipe in a vertical position the way it would be on a real diesel truck. By the time Robbie was finished, his truck had sides, a roof, a seat for the driver, thumb tacks for head lights, rear lights, and side lights. It even had several small pieces of paper glued to the back on which he had the teacher write some numbers. "It's got to have quite a few licenses 'cause it's a cross country truck."

Robbie had been helped to stick to his job, to develop his span of concentration, and to put more thought into his work, to get more satisfaction out of it. And he received this sort of help over and over, but needing less and less of it each time, until he had really learned better working habits. The whole group was impressed with Robbie's work and that was another satisfaction to him.

He used his truck on the block highways that were built in the classroom day after day. He stopped at someone's gasoline station for gas. He delivered "furniture" and "freight" to some of the children who had "stores" and "houses" of blocks. His truck was kept in school on the shelves near the block shelves, where everyone's work bench products were kept till the end of the school year, to be used in the group play by Robbie and by others to whom he loaned it. Robbie's truck was in this way a means of teaching him also the pleasures of group play and co-operation.

THE TEACHER TEACHES THE CHILDREN THE BEGINNINGS OF GOOD SOCIAL LIVING

It is obvious that the teacher is teaching her children many things at the same time. As they are living and working together in school, they are learning how to get along with other children. Now children learn how to get along with others in some fashion wherever they are thrown in with others, whether it be the city playground, the unsupervised empty lot, the back yard with Mother looking out the window occasionally. But *what* each child learns about getting on with others depends on the temperament and past experiences of the other children and the adults (if any) who are with him. In many instances he may be learning social techniques that are unfriendly and that may even be a hinderance to him later as he grows up into a world where friendly interdependence is becoming more and more essential if civilization is to survive. Some of his social techniques may have to be unlearned and new ones acquired when he enters a nursery group. The little boy with the bullying older brother, whom we have already described, had to unlearn in school his tense and defensive methods of getting on at home, and under the teacher's guidance become accustomed to a more relaxed and constructive give and take with people of his own age. (Part of the teacher's job here was to get to know his parents well and to help them understand some of the feelings of that older brother.) The teacher feels pretty sure that if the children who are in her group today are to be responsible, intelligent, and friendly citizens in the world of tomorrow they will get a good start by having a happy and satisfying group life at nursery school.

By Redirecting Asocially Directed Energies
Into Socially Acceptable Activities

She will need to help them very gradually to accept the modifications of their behavior that are required by group living and that are possible for them at their stage of development. She will allow the children a great deal of freedom to find their own best ways of getting on with others. She will give positive encouragement to friendly and sensible social techniques. She will, of course, need to forbid some of the antisocial behavior, and the children would not feel secure with her unless they were sure that she would forbid it and help them control their strong primitive drives. When the teacher forbids one way of acting, she does not forbid the emotional feeling or the ideas behind it. As has already been stated, she accepts the child and all his feelings,

ideas, and energies. But she suggests alternative ways of expressing the same feelings or ideas, ways that are more socially accepted. For example, the little boy with the older brother was forbidden to sock the other children indiscriminately, but he was encouraged to work at the work bench where his aggressive energies had a constructive outlet, and where, eventually, he would learn the pleasures of turning out products that he could use with the other children, such as Robbie's truck. This area of teaching is what people usually call discipline. We can see that "discipline" in nursery school is guidance towards self-discipline and self-control. These are qualities that are very essential in a democratic society where an adult is supposed to be able to control himself as well as to think for himself without being told how to do so by any dictator except his own common sense and his own warm and civilized feelings.

Different Children Need Different Social Teachings

The teacher will need to teach some children to be more free, some to be more controlled. The little girl who comes to school afraid to touch the clay because she has been told she shouldn't get dirty, or the scissors because she has been told she might hurt herself, needs freedom at school to counter-balance the terrific limitations she has previously experienced. The little boy who is anxious because he is allowed to do anything at all at home (and yet he knows the adults there don't really like all that they let him do) is helped by gentle but firm guidance into constructive activities at school. He may very possibly splash the water all around the bathroom with wild and excited abandon in his play or when he is washing. The teacher might forbid this to continue for very long and help him to wash cars and doll clothes, to discover how the 'water wheel works, to blow soap bubbles, and to engage in any of the many enjoyable but constructive things one can do with water.

It Takes Time to Enlarge One's Circle of Friends

As we have seen, the child's social life started with his baby dependence on his mother. Through her loving attention to his physical needs she drew his developing feelings of love away from himself and toward her. Since that time he has also extended friendly feelings to his father, his brothers and sisters, other relatives and friends, and now to the teacher. But most two-year-olds, many threes, and even some fours are not ready to extend many friendly feelings to the other children in the nursery school group when they first come to school. It is hard to share the teacher, your new found friend, with all these other children. This is why nursery school groups are kept small, so that the teacher and her assistants will really be able to build up the close relationship with the children that we have been describing. The teacher will need to show each child that she can take care of him and of all the other children too. She will not only show him this by her actions, but she will occasionally need to say it to him in words, as Maggie's teacher did with her. And then she must listen to the child and try to see whether there is any real cause for the child's continuing jealousy that she can remove. Actually the teacher, like the mother, cannot avoid having children feel jealous, but she can help them to live through it and come out with positive friendly feelings eventually. Gradually, as the children live with this teacher and this group they become more and more aware of the teacher's interest in each child, and because they love and admire her, they gradually act as she does. They develop the beginnings of sympathy, generosity, considerate helpfulness, a sense of justice, and other feelings that one hopes adults will have in good measure.

By Helping Personal Contacts be Socially Acceptable

A teacher does a good deal of interpreting of one child to another. For instance, when a two-year-old tries to help another child put on his hat, the chances are that his awkward coordination will seem like rough handling compared to the gentle ease of an adult. The second child may fuss and draw back with fear from the child who wishes to do what the teacher is doing. If this is to be a situation where these two will learn the joys of social living, it must be a successful situation. So the teacher calls over from where she is dressing another child, "Edny just wants to help you, Peter. Edny, Peter likes you to do it very gently." Her calm slow voice is reassuring, but with two-year-olds the bodily presence of the adult is even a greater reassurance. So she moves over, helps Edny get the hat on straight, smiles reassuringly at Peter, and helps him bear up under all this, and then beams at both. "Isn't Edny a good helper!" she says to Peter. Both children beam at each other with real interest. They have taken one step in learning how to get along together happily and cooperatively.

The teacher finds herself using language and a friendly tone of voice (both of which she *can* use with so much greater facility than can the children) to help them understand each other and themselves.

"Betsy needs that one now"—to a child who is trying to take a shovel away from someone else. "Here's another one for you." Children cannot learn to share willingly what they have not had sufficient opportunity to investigate, manipulate, and use for themselves first. So the nursery school is well-stocked with duplicate materials.

"It's his turn now, Ann. Sandy, you finish up your swing quickly because you've had a long turn. Then it will be Ann's turn."

About a crying child, "She fell and bumped her knee and I'm fixing it so it will be all right."

To two four-year-olds (who are attracted to where one of their friends is saying vehemently to the teacher, "You're an old skunk, that's what you are. A stinky skunk") the teacher says, "Sonny's angry at me because I won't let him lasso Angela. Angela does not want to be lassoed." Angela was one of the tiniest and weakest in the class. The two friends are interested and have listened with a glint of pleasure to Sonny's tirade. The teacher continues, "I suggested that Sonny lasso the sawhorses or the barrels, but Sonny's really very angry at me now." She smiles a little mischievously at Sonny, who has calmed down a bit. He says, "I'm glad you smiled." She continues smiling at Sonny as she says, "You know, we could make some real heads for those sawhorses out of cardboard. And what could we use for tails?" The two friends are interested in this project, although Sonny is still not completely happy, because, as he had already told the teacher, "Sawhorses don't move." However, he follows along with his friends and is eventually carried away by their enthusiasm in fixing up the sawhorses and lassoing them.

By Allowing Freedom for Social Interaction Within Broad Limits That the Teacher Sets to Help the Children with Their Social Living

The teacher stands for law and order and fairness to all. She leaves the children free to carry on their play and work independently of her and to settle their own difficulties in so far as they are able. But she stands ready to help them out before they become angrily over-excited or unhappily frustrated. If there is a situation where fisticuffs or hair-pulling or wild fighting is about to be engaged in, she averts this. For she knows that children do not learn anything positive from the high excitement and the fear both of what their assailant might do to them and what they, in their uncontrolled state, might do to their assailant. They will learn from this a feeling of excitement and fear and even terror. But how much better for them to learn the feeling of grown-upness that comes with being able to settle a disagreement by compromising the way adults do (at least idealistically they wish to). Children will be angry even if they compromise, but it will be easier to cool off if real injury has not been added to insult. And the teacher may provide, besides the work bench, a punching bag, a target at which to throw or kick balls, and other harmless ways of letting off one's anger without learning overwhelming guilt and fear.

Some children need her help in social situations for a long time before they feel the security in themselves that comes from having lived through many social crises successfully. Were the teacher to withdraw her support and push a child off to fight his own battles before he feels capable of doing so, she would be teaching him, first, that adults are not very helpful or understanding people. They really don't care what happens to other people. Secondly, he would be learning to fight his own battles, either by retreating passively and keeping out of trouble fearfully, or by taking the offensive and being perpetually on guard, or in some other way that carries with it the hidden dependence and fear that he has not been allowed to show. This feeling of dependence and fear and immaturity may quite possibly continue with him throughout life and be a force within him that he must keep struggling to hide, especially from himself. How much better that his teacher should satisfy his need for help toward more social behavior while he is young, and thereby teach him to achieve gradually a real and mature independence with her support.

By Helping Children Utilize Group Situations

As has been shown the teacher teaches good social living by her interest in the children's play and by a word spoken here or a piece of equipment suggested there. One group of "young threes" had a group game that they enjoyed immensely. It started one day when the teacher heard a little girl who was sitting under a wooden platform in the school room saying cheerfully, "It's raining ev'ybody." Nobody had heard, so the teacher copied her words and tones, only louder, "It's raining everybody, Cathy says." The children looked up, looking out the window first (no rain) then catching on by Cathy's smile, that this was pretend. About six children huddled with her under the platform, all happily saying, "It's raining." Several days later this was repeated, but now the group knew about the game and enjoyed being together in it, and did not need any help from the teacher. Once the teacher started singing with them "Rain is Falling Down", a song they all knew. And at the end one little boy said, smiling, "Rain is falling up." The teacher entered his joke by smiling with him, since none of his friends "got it." The teacher never laughs *at* her children when she is in school,

but she often laughs with them. She comes to understand the very simple direct humor of children and enjoys it with them.

By Guiding Children to an Understanding
of the Values of Each Child to the Group

The teacher is teaching the children, mostly by the way she herself treats individuals and sometimes by directly calling their attention to it, that everybody in their group enriches the group life in one way or another. Josie, almost five, certainly has a hard time sitting still for even a short discussion. The group is often disturbed by her, since she wants to do all the talking or else leave. But she can draw beautifully. One child is building a zoo of blocks and, while he asks the teacher what he can use for "wild animals", she suggests that maybe Josie could make him some animals of paper because she draws so well. This is satisfactory to the child and to Josie, and, because Josie's crayoned

and cut-out animals are quite remarkable and are admired by all, she feels pretty important in the group, important enough to be a little "steadier" during the next discussion period.

The children are learning the real values in people. The cheerful, thoughtful expression of George's face is of importance to you, not the color of that face. The fact that he has good ideas for your play together is of more importance to you than whether he is shorter or taller, fatter or thinner than you, or whether his father goes to the same church your father goes to or to no church at all, or even whether he believes in Santa Claus or not.

By Providing Opportunities for Responsibility

The children are learning to take the responsibility for doing certain small jobs around the classroom that need to be done every day: jobs such as watering the plants, feeding the salamanders, wiping off and setting the tables for lunch, helping get out and put away their cots. The older children like to go into the classroom of the younger children to help serve lunch to them if they eat at a different time. The children enjoy doing these "grown-up" jobs and the teacher arranges that each may have his turn.

By Including Some Group Times in Her Daily Schedule

There are several times during the day when the children come together as a group. Children are always taking off or putting on their hats and coats at the same time. In the middle of the morning all sit down to a snack-together, and again at lunch-time if the school provides the mid-day meal. Rest time is a group affair. So is music time, usually story time, trips, discussions, and the group games and activities that spring up from certain interests at certain times. With the youngest children these group times tend to be short (except, of course, the mid-day rest) and not everybody joins the group. The older the children become, the longer they can stay together in enjoyable group times. These give the children the opportunity to observe the teacher in relation to the whole group. They observe her interests, not only in what they have to contribute to the discussion, but also in the contributions of the other children. They notice her enthusiasm in playing the game that some child has suggested. This is one way in which their interest in all the other children is strengthened and in which their common interests are carried forward by the teacher.

By Helping Children Learn That, Although They Don't Like Everyone, They Can Live Socially with Everyone

Thus, the teacher is teaching the children in various ways that there are many children of one's own age whom it is fun to be with and to do things with; that things are more fun when you and the other children take turns with equipment, accept each other's ideas for play, settle your difficulties by trying to compromise and reach a mutually satisfactory way of getting on. The children also are learning that one doesn't like everyone one's own age equally well, but that even if you don't like somebody, you can still get along with him. You may just happen not to play with somebody much. He doesn't seem to catch on to every-

The older the children become, the
longer they can stay together in
enjoyable group times. These give
the children the opportunity to observe
the teacher in relation to the whole
group.

thing you suggest or talk about or he doesn't seem to do the same sort of things you do. You may come to admit that he does have certain good points, like bringing candy to school to share with everybody after lunch or making all those different sorts of block buildings. Eventually you may find yourself playing in his block building with him and having a good time.

Children in nursery school are learning in many ways that their own life in the group is most satisfactory when the life of everyone else in the group is also going along well.

THE TEACHER INCREASES HER CHILDREN'S INTEREST IN AND UNDERSTANDING OF THEIR IMMEDIATE WORLD

A further large area that the nursery school teacher is covering in her instruction is that of broadening and deepening her group's understanding of the world around them. The only part of the world that has any real meaning to young children is that part that is very close to them spatially and temporally. The teacher restricts her instruction to this area.

Talk and Pictures Alone Not a Satisfactory Method of Instruction

Although she could talk with the children about the forests where our lumber comes from, for instance, or the sort of country where the elephants live, and the children would be interested and would talk about it, their talk would of necessity be based on repeating what the teacher had said as they had connected this in their thinking with past experiences they had had. Since they would not have had any firsthand experience with forests and with elephant country, that is, any opportunity to see, to hear, to smell, to touch, to walk around in them (unless, of course, these were children living in such a locality) their thinking about them would be hazy. Pictures would be a help. But even pictures might be misleading, as a New York teacher found with her Allen. Allen was five. He had heard those children in his group, who had been on farms in the summer, talk about cows. Those children had talked about their experiences at the group discussion times, and the teacher had read several stories about cows and showed pictures of barns and cows. Allen was very fond of animals. He liked to feed the school rabbit and play

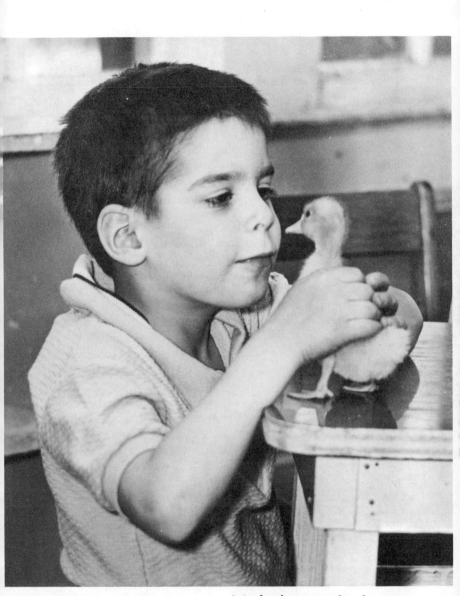

A further large area that the nursery school teacher is covering in her instruction is that of broadening and deepening her group's understanding of the world around them.

43

with it. One day the teacher was chatting with him about the barn he was making of blocks. He was building "stanchions" for his "cows", and some of his remarks make the teacher ask, "How big are the cows anyway?" Allen sat back on his heels. Apparently he had not thought of this particular point before. He said, "About as big as that rabbit." The teacher did not correct his impression then, but when they took a trip to the stable several weeks later, she asked some of the children who had seen cows whether cows were bigger or smaller than these horses. She made sure that Allen heard them say, "Just as long and not quite so high." This helped Allen adjust his imaginary cow to a more realistic size.

The Teacher Encourages Children to Think

Now what, if anything, is wrong with children having imaginary ideas that are hazy? Actually, there is nothing wrong in their having *some* such ideas. And no matter how much we lead young children to observe the realities around them, they will have some fantastic ideas about this reality because of their lack of experience with it. As we have said, imagining is one way in which a child copes with his experience and stretches his thinking abilities. The teacher allows him free expression for it. She did not squelch Allen and make him feel inferior just because his experience with words and pictures had not taught him the size of a cow. No, the teacher wants to teach children to think. Therefore, she respects their efforts at thinking and encourages them in these efforts. At the same time she presents them with first-hand experiences that will help them clarify their thinking and understand better the real relationships between one thing and another.

Because, if it is true that we wish to produce adults who will take a thoughtful and responsibly active interest in the life of their community and of the world at large, we must start teaching them as children to think as clearly and thoroughly and honestly as possible and to discriminate, as they gain experience, between what is real and what is unreal. We do not wish them to stop fantasying altogether, but we wish them to come to know *when* they are fantasying. And if a child begins to withdraw into fantasy and away from active interest in the real life around him, it is generally an indication that the real world is somehow not pleasurable enough to him, and that he and his family need help to make it more so.

For most normally developing children are naturally interested in their immediate environment and wish to investigate and find out about it. They are constantly figuring out relationships between an object and its name, an object and its characteristic ways of behaving, things and what you can do with them, people and what they do, causes and effects, and many more. They immediately sense that the teacher approves of this intellectual curiosity of theirs. She has provided them with equipment to use and experiment with. She helps them to understand each other. She is actively interested in the same things the children are interested in, and because of her greater experience, is in a position to expose them to new situations in which they can learn more about these same things in which they are already interested.

The Teacher Provides First-Hand Experiences as a Scientific Approach to Learning

In Allen's class of four-and-a-halfs through fives there was a general interest in animals. The children who had been to the country talked a good deal about country animals. The teacher wished to give the group an experience with city animals, so that everyone could participate in the discussions with a greater fund of first-hand information. So they took a trip to the home of one of the teachers to see a family of kittens with the mother cat. The teacher brought a pet rabbit into school and kept it in the classroom. They noticed animals on the street. Some of the children started to play horse. One little girl built a fine house for her rubber horse, covered him with blankets at night, fed him chocolate pudding out of a dish and treated him as any good mother would treat her child. Many of the children played at feeding and caring for horses. They played they were pulling a laundry wagon like Porkchops (formerly a butcher's horse) who passed school every day. The teacher planned with a nearby stable manager a trip to his stable. She saw from their play that these children were interested in what horses eat, where they sleep, what sort of work they do. She did not care so much that they must get their facts straight about how these processes take place. What she did care about was that the children were obviously interested in these processes, and that this sort of an excursion would broaden their real experience with horses. If after the trip, the little girl still got great pleasure from building her toy horse a doll bed and covering him over with blankets, well, that would be perfectly all right.

And the teacher would not expect any child to take in a specific list of facts on any trip. The children are free to observe those things that have a special interest for them. The teacher is alert to all they are passing and to the children's remarks and what they are observing. She may pause and draw their attention to what one child has noticed or to something that she feels is relevant to their thinking and to the concepts she is hoping they are building. "Johnny sees something on top of this building, don't you Johnny. What is it?" "A flag." Teacher, "I wonder why it flaps about like that." A child, "The wind is blowing it." Then there is more observation of the wind's action. They point to the direction it is blowing toward and then the direction it is coming from. They lick a finger and hold it up. They look at a cloud blow by as they proceed on their way to the stable.

The teacher also sets a pattern of friendliness and good manners, so that, when she appreciatively thanks Mr. I, the stableman, upon leaving, many of the children copy her and know that she approves of their doing so. While they are on the trip, the teacher may remind the children of things they have wanted to find out about horses. She may pose questions that require the children to use their senses more fully, as on this same stable trip, when they came in and found only wagons on the street floor, she said, "I wonder where the horses are?" "I can smell them", said several. "That's right", encouraged the teacher. "I hear them", said several, as the horses on the second floor stomped their hooves, "They're upstairs."

The teacher is really teaching a scientific method of investigation. She never sets herself up as the final authority who knows everything. Often she asks, "How could we find out?" Often she herself needs to read up about trains, airplanes, science and so on. Often they take several trips to the same place. Children welcome trips. They feel pleased that they are being included in the adult world around them. They have the chance to talk on a man-to-man basis with adults who are doing work that is important. The teacher has already prepared the adult involved to be simple in his explanations to the children. Here are other people to strengthen the child's idea of an adult as a person who does interesting work. They find out some of the simple details of how he does that work. With the stableman they found out how he gets the hay down from the loft, how he pitches it into the stall (they learned in their muscles how heavy a pitch fork of hay is by trying to lift it), how he scatters the bedding around, how he gives each horse his oats, how he curries him with the curry comb. Then the children go back to school. Often they digest a trip for a while without doing anything about it. Then they start reenacting it in their play and talking about it.

The Teacher Encourages Intellectual Curiosity and Intellectual Honesty

Sometimes the children's curiosities need to be satisfied with very simple, honest statements. For instance, when the child asks the teacher, "How does the baby get out from inside his mother?" the teacher wishes to give the child an honest answer and be sure that it is in agreement with what his mother has told him or will tell him. She may ask him, "How do *you* think?" or "How does your mommy say?" until she finds out from the mother what she has told him. If the teacher wishes to say it differently, she explains to the mother why she does. If a child is trying to solve a problem and needs our help on it, we are of most educational value to him if we respect his intelligence and help him with his problem. And we also show him that we like his growing up and his expanding mental inquisitiveness.

In other words the teacher is being as honest with him in his search for knowledge in the world about him as she is in helping him to find out about himself and his own abilities and emotions and feelings. She did not cover up the fact that Sonny was angry with her. It was obvious that he was and why he was, and she was not disturbed by it. When a child bumps his knee, she says with honesty, "That hurts, doesn't it? Let's wash it off. It will be O.K. in a jiffy." When Alice (4½ years) was playing with the new doll in the doll corner and Sandra approached her looking as though she wanted to play with it too, Alice said, as she had heard others outside of school say, "Go away. I don't like little colored girls." The teacher pointed out to Alice that she had wanted Sandra to go away, not because she was a colored girl, but because she looked as though she wanted the doll. She then suggested that maybe Sandra could be the aunt in this house, since Alice was the mother, and that was acceptable to both children. The teacher wants the child to face the reality of his own feelings—his "good" ones and his "bad" ones, although she never calls them bad.

The World is a Very Interesting Place

With two-year-olds the discoveries about the world go on for the most part right within the classroom with perhaps an occasional trip to the kitchen, if it is very close, or to the nurse's office on their floor. They look up at the clouds and smoke. They feel ice and snow and taste a good bit of it. They watch the water going down the pipes in the basin and toilet. And somebody usually has the bright idea to look under the basin and see the pipes. After many days of investigation several children realize that the warm pipe leads up to the warm water faucet and the cool one up to the cold water faucet. Just turning on and off the faucets at two is adventure aplenty. And the teacher supervises this experience, as she does others, to prevent any frightening occurrences, such as getting burned by too hot water or being scared by too great a rush of water. Frightening experiences might diminish the child's desire to find out.

At three one's horizon is a little wider. "Who empties the scrapbaskets?" asks a three-year-old. The teacher arranges with the handy man to visit the class. "This is Jo and Jo empties the scrapbasket. Jo would you have time to show us where you empty the scrapbasket?" Jo chats with the children as they take the scrapbasket down to the basement and empty it. He tells them how he puts the big trash can up on the sidewalk. Another day they watch the trash collection truck come by and collect trash. Another day they take a broken chair to Jo in his work shop and watch as he mends it. Now they feel they have another good friend and they have observed two work processes that vitally affect their group life.

Another group of threes was interested in the elevated train that they could see at the end of the street from school. On one trip they walked underneath it to get a better view and listen to its noise. On a second trip they sat on the station platform and watched. "How do they know everybody is in? How do they know to shut the doors?" There was a little fear that somebody might be left out. So they watched people getting in and out. They saw how watchful the conductor was. This was not the rush hour. On a third trip they actually got on the El and rode from one stop to the next, a matter of six blocks.

The four-year-olds in this same school took a longer trip on the El. They noticed many more things, such as signals, the levers for opening and closing the doors, the switches in the tracks and so on.

Fours who have been in a nursery school group before and have learned about the world of the nursery school room are ready for a good many trips outside it. They find in their discussions with the teacher that there are many places in the school that they want to find out more about: the school kitchen with its large cold ice boxes, large hot stoves, steaming dish washer, great stirring machines, and the friendly cook who prepares their meals; the furnace room and the coal bins; the telephone switchboard and the offices. Outside the building they watch the snow removal, go to the store and buy the food they need for their own cooking, watch new buildings going up, streets being repaired, cars being repaired and refueled at the gas station. The teacher, as has been said, knows the community and is prepared with ideas for appropriate excursions as the interests arise. Part of the reason why they arise is that the teacher is herself alert to what is going on about her, not only on the child's level, but on an adult level. She does not subject the child to adult problems. But because she is a wide-awake, interested person herself, she can be honestly responsive to what the children are interested in.

The Nursery School Teacher Teaches the Beginnings of Some Academic Subjects

Now what about the academic subjects, the three Rs and others. Actually, the foundations are being laid for later work in these. The most important parts of that foundation are all the learnings that we have already been discussing: the child's

The teacher chooses many good
books. She places them on low
shelves where the children can get
them whenever they want them.

good relationship with his teacher and through this his growing understanding of himself, his feelings 'and his abilities; his maturing social techniques; his developing skills with language, with thought, and with materials; his widening and deepening interest in the world about him and his more capable organization of his knowledge about it and of his methods of finding out about it.

Geography

So far as geography is concerned he has a beginning of map-thinking gained from taking trips and getting to know the layout of his immediate vicinity. The river is in that direction, the stores are this way. He is helped by the teacher to carry this sense of direction inside the school building with him. He may, especially as he gets on toward five years of age, be able to reproduce streets and buildings in his block schemes. This becomes a sort of map. At five years of age the whole group occasionally plans, builds, and plays on such a map. A child is, also, throughout his nursery school experience, gaining a knowledge of how weather and the earth affect men's living. If he is near an airport he sees the effect of fog on the activities there. If he was in New York City or its suburbs during a summer of drought, he began with the teacher's simplifications of the matter and her guidance toward observation, to notice the lack of rain and to notice its effect on gardens, dirty cars, and his family's concern with water conservation at home. He is beginning to observe how man has coped with nature. Here is a big bay between several cities. People have made bridges and ferries and barges and lighters and so on to get themselves and their goods across. All of this is geography.

Arithmetic

Mathematics gets an important start in pre-school years. The child is building up mathematical concepts as he builds with blocks. "These two here are just as long as this one on the opposite side. He compares two pieces of wood and saws one off to be the same length as the other so he will have two even sides for his truck. For the "fours" the teacher sometimes enlivens the putting-away time by a sort of number game. "Here are two blocks, and here is one more. And now how many do you have?" The children are interested in comparing the weights of things, not the numerical weights, but the feel of the weight in their muscles. A simple balance scale provides a way of checking whether one thing is heavier or lighter than another. Cooking requires the use of liquid measure. Again it is not the actual terminology of measuring that the teacher is after, although it becomes evident that it makes a big difference in the sort of junket you get, whether you have put in one cup of milk or two or three. But the experience of actually pouring liquids from one container to another, and the comparison of sizes of containers, and the estimation of whether something is a large volume or not, weighs more or not—these are the concepts the teacher wishes her children to become interested in as they play.

The children are, of course, interested in counting and do a good deal of it in relation to setting out the number of chairs they need, the number of places for lunch, etc.: Those who are most interested in numbers enjoy such games as dominoes and parchesi played in a very simple way.

Reading and Other Language Skills

How about the language arts—reading, writing, English composition, grammar, etc.? The nursery school teacher first of all encourages her children to experiment with language, as she has encouraged them to experiment with and develop skill in the use of their other muscles and senses and of the art media which she has presented to them. She enjoys with them their efforts to copy sounds they hear, to invent sounds that amuse or interest them. A four-year-old is describing a steam shovel. "Tchk, tchk, tchk. The smoke comes out that little pipe betord the back." The teacher tries in many ways to help the child keep the creative approach to language with which he has started his baby vocalizing, at the same time that he is copying the adults and children about him and is developing a larger vocabulary and more complicated syntax. She tries to use simple but vivid language herself in talking to the children. She uses good grammar herself, and in her own speech she may emphasize, or even overemphasize, the correct sentence structure of sentences the children frequently mispronounce. "We don't have *any* more pencils," said with great dramatic fervor to a group whose

The teacher . . . reads to the children every day. She picks many stories that deal directly with the things the children are interested in, and she reads these to the children after they have taken a trip or had an interesting experience together. . .

members say to her, "I don't got no pencil." She makes up games that will use the sounds and words and structures the children need to practice in a correct form. The children are helped toward better grammar and pronunciation by listening to her and other adults and by trying out what they hear.

The teacher writes down stories that they tell at group times or individually. By the time they are four, getting on toward five, they are interested in hearing these stories read back to them and in collecting them into a group book. Maybe they make several books—one about boats, one about animals, and so on. The child realizes that the teacher thinks his language is interesting and good and this helps him build up a healthy respect for it himself and encourages his creative use of it. If this approach to language can be maintained in his early school years, it will help him not only in English composition but in all his school subjects.

The teacher chooses many good books. She places them on low shelves where the children can get them whenever they want them. She reads to the children every day. She picks many stories that deal directly with the things the children are interested in, and she reads these to the children *after* they have taken a trip or had an interesting experience together and after they have discussed their experiences. In this way the story helps to pull together and clarify children's thinking, but it does not give them ready-made images or ready-made language. They are free to observe in their own unique way and to use their own efforts in thinking about their experience and talking about it. Then they can listen to the words of the story with their own real images in their mind. In other words, the language they are hearing is meaningful to them. It is vitally important that children have a store of experiences and a meaningful vocabulary by the time they start learning how to read at six. This sort of a background helps prepare them for quick comprehension of what they are reading.

An interest in written symbols is developing in the children through having many suitable books easily accessible to them. Also they ask the teacher to write signs for their block buildings. "Main Street," "Smith's Grocery Store," "Lumber Yard," or a more complicated sign such as, "Nobody can come in unless they are not an enemy." Four-year-olds can read their own names printed in correct manuscript (not all capitals) on their coat cubbies, cots, washrag hooks, and on the committee chart, if they have one. Twos and threes usually have a colored ribbon or a small picture as the symbol that marks their cubbie. Fours enjoy playing various symbol games, such as picture lotto and animal lotto, in which it is necessary to match one picture with a similar one. This matching of symbols will, of course, go on mentally in reading, when it will be groups of letters or sounds instead of pictures to remember and match. Five-year-olds start noticing signs along the streets and roads, such as "Stop," "Go," "School Bus Stop", "No Parking" and so on. They enjoy it when the teacher makes identical signs for their use at school, such as the "Danger, Men at Work" sign that some fours requested from their teacher. They set it up in front of the place where they were digging in the earth. It helped them in their identification with real workmen, as did the caps they had gotten from the dressup chest and the real trench shovels that their teacher had bought at an Army surplus store. In all these ways the teacher might be said to be teaching reading readiness.

As the children are encouraged to talk freely, to experiment with language, to use it for expressing their thought, they are, of course gaining facility in using it as a tool for social communication. Language develops through the child's relationship with his mother. The teacher also is an interested listener to what the child has to say to her. She really looks at him when he is talking to her and responds with understanding and with language of her own that he can understand. As we have seen, she helps him in his talking to other people when he needs it and she helps others in talking to him. She helps children express their feelings and their desires in words, so that they can understand each other better and get along together better.

If a child stutters or persists in immature pronunciation, or is delayed in speaking at all, the teacher tries to make him feel as comfortable with her as possible. She does not harrass him or increase his tension by correcting him. She helps him to be active and expressive in those ways that he can be—perhaps in painting, in rhythms, at the work bench. She talks with the parents a good deal in an effort to understand him better. If his problem persists, she probably discusses with his mother the advisability of her getting some psychiatric advice on the difficulty.

SUMMARY

The child in nursery school is taught more than all these things. For instance, he is taught specific songs and games in music. But his learnings have taken place in the general areas discussed. The teacher has been teaching him to develop as an individual and as a group member at the same time. Her teaching is founded on an affectionate, understanding relationship with each child. It has taken the form of guidance, by choosing certain equipment, by arranging a schedule of group and free activities and quiet and lively activities, by giving much understanding approval, some understanding disapproval, by willing help and substitute activities where needed. To summarize briefly, the teacher has tried to teach the child:

That school is another place, besides home, where one can feel cared for and protected and secure.

That adults, like the teacher, are gentle, helpful and loving people, that they are fair and just, that they are interested in people and in the world around them, that they are active and informed, that they like materials and tools and the children's products, etc.

That he (the child) is a worthwhile and competent individual and group member. That he can use his body and mind with developing ease.

To become aware of himself—of his body and what he can do with it, of his feelings and desires and how he can express them and act on them in socially accepted ways.

To become a good worker—constructive, thoughtful, concentrated, respectful of tools, interested in and pleased with creative effort and the results of it.

Increasing ability to enjoy living in a group, to contribute to a group, to form pleasurable friendships, and to accept the modifications of one's behavior that a group requires.

A greater awareness of and understanding of the world around him—a method of first-hand investigation—a greater basis of reality for his thinking on the relationship of one thing to another.

A foundation for academic work in school.